DATE DUE

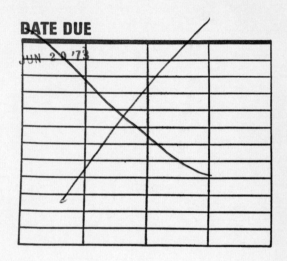

JUN 20 '73

THE MODERN POETS SERIES   William J. Martz, General Editor

THE ACHIEVEMENT OF THEODORE ROETHKE

A COMPREHENSIVE SELECTION OF HIS POEMS WITH A CRITICAL INTRODUCTION

WILLIAM J. MARTZ
Ripon College

SCOTT, FORESMAN AND COMPANY

for **NED**

Books by Theodore Roethke

OPEN HOUSE. New York, Knopf, 1941.

THE LOST SON AND OTHER POEMS. Garden City, New York, Doubleday, 1948.

PRAISE TO THE END! Garden City, New York, Doubleday, 1951.

THE WAKING: POEMS 1933-1953. Garden City, New York, Doubleday, 1953.

THE COLLECTED VERSE OF THEODORE ROETHKE: WORDS FOR THE WIND. Garden City, New York, Doubleday, 1958; Indiana University Press, 1961.

I AM! SAYS THE LAMB. Garden City, New York, Doubleday, 1961.

SEQUENCE, SOMETIMES METAPHYSICAL. Iowa City, Stone Wall Press, 1963.

THE FAR FIELD. Garden City, New York, Doubleday, 1964.

ON THE POET AND HIS CRAFT: SELECTED PROSE OF THEODORE ROETHKE. Edited by Ralph J. Mills, Jr., Seattle, University of Washington Press, 1965.

CONTENTS

THEODORE ROETHKE (1908-1963)

Theodore Roethke was born on May 25, 1908, in Saginaw, Michigan and grew up in the environment of a greenhouse owned by his father and uncle. He received his B.A. from the University of Michigan in 1929 and his M.A. in 1936. He taught at Lafayette College, Pennsylvania State College, and Bennington College and, from 1947 until his death, at the University of Washington, where his reputation as a distinguished teacher crystallized. In 1953 he married Beatrice Heath O' Connell (O' Connell's daughter in "The Shy Man"), who had been a student at Bennington when he was teaching there. They had no children.

Roethke's many honors, comprehending all major awards given in poetry in the United States, include Guggenheim Fellowships in 1946 and 1950, the Pulitzer Prize in 1954 for *The Waking: Poems, 1933-1953*, the 1958 Bollingen Prize and the 1959 Edna St. Vincent Millay Prize for *Words for the Wind*, a two-year Ford Foundation Fellowship awarded in 1959, and posthumously the National Book Award in 1965 for *The Far Field*.

In addition to being both a distinguished poet and teacher, Theodore Roethke was also an outstanding oral interpreter of his own poetry. His reading of his own poems — *Words for the Wind: Selections from the Poetry of Theodore Roethke* (Folkways, FL 9736) — is distinctive and moving.

A MAJOR AMERICAN POET

A striking characteristic of the poetry of Theodore Roethke is its relation to the romantic tradition. "I proclaim once more a condition of joy,"[1]
he announces, after Wordsworth. "O to be delivered from the rational
into the realm of pure song,"[2] he exclaims, and the reader thinks of
Keats' immortal Bird not born for death but singing of summer in full-
throated ease, or of Shelley's skylark pouring from near Heaven a full
heart in profuse strains of unpremeditated art.

In a typically romantic way Roethke speaks for individuality: "I saw
the separateness of all things";[3] and in a typically romantic way he is anti-
rational: "Reason? That dreary shed, that hutch for grubby schoolboys!"[4]
"We think by feeling."[5] When we hear him assert, "And I became
all that I looked upon,"[6] we remember Whitman's child who went forth
every day "And the first object he look'd upon, that object he became."
"We come to something without knowing why"[7] again recalls the voice
of Whitman, "There is that in me—I do not know what it is—but I know
it is in me";[8] and of course it is recalled by Roethke's own invocation,
"Be with me, Whitman, maker of catalogues: / For the world invades
me again."[9]

Comparisons of Roethke with other romantic poets could be multiplied
indefinitely—in the twentieth century with, for example, E. E. Cummings'
persistent song of joy, "may my heart always be open to little / birds who
are the secrets of living" or with Cummings' anti-rational "let's live
suddenly without thinking." But finally it is toward the later Yeats, as
toward Whitman, that Roethke turns: "I take this cadence from a man
named Yeats . . . Yes, I was dancing-mad and how / That came to be the
bears and Yeats would know."[10] Roethke, "dancing-mad" and "self-
enchanted," has an implicit epigraph for all his poems in the last lines of
the last poem in his last book: "And everything comes to One, / As we
dance on, dance on, dance on."

But the fact that Roethke relates to the romantic tradition not only invites us to see him as part of that tradition but also forces us to ask whether
he is able to absorb that tradition in terms of his own *originality*. We may
wince at the proclamation of a condition of joy not because we oppose

---

[1]"I Cry Love! Love!" (Footnotes 1–10, 12–18, and 21–23 refer to the poems from which lines are ex-
cerpted.)   [2]"What Can I Tell My Bones?"   [3]"A Field of Light."   [4]"I Cry Love! Love!"   [5]"The
Waking."   [6]"I Waited."   [7]"The Manifestation."   [8]"Song of Myself," line 1309.   [9]"The
Abyss."   [10]"Four for Sir John Davies."

the idea but rather because we oppose what is now the staleness of the expression of the idea. Closely linked to the question of originality is inevitably the question of the depth or the comprehensiveness of Roethke's experience, that is, the depth of his experience as it is comprehended in his poems. To take *originality* and *depth* as criteria for responding to Roethke is to inquire about his *style*. *Style* is an omnibus term, relentlessly elusive in the face of analysis, yet we know that, writing in the romantic tradition, Roethke can absorb that tradition; he can have his own style.

So, not to give needless emphasis to the metaphysics of poetry criticism, our question becomes, What is there about Roethke's style—his voice as a poet—that makes us decline easy definition? The general answers to such a question are widely known in our own age of literary criticism; for example, we know that a good poet structures a poem with care, that in one way or another he will use metaphor or symbol, and that his rhythms are crucial to the final effect he seeks. But the specific answers take us on something of a "journey to the interior" (the archetypal metaphor is the title of one of the poems in Roethke's ambitious "North American Sequence"[11]). The interior is on the one hand the interior of the poem, where the poem takes us in terms of an exploration of human experience, and on the other hand the interior of ourselves, where we take the poem, our capacity for response.

To experience the poems of Roethke, to go to their interior, requires an awareness of the fact that he is persistently in the act of wishing—with, of course, many gradations in his wishing, though intensity, or yearning, is characteristic: "Let Light attend me to the grave!"[12] "And willingly would I dispense / With false accouterments of sense"[13]—note the key *would I;* "Enshroud me with Light! O Whirling! O Terrible Love!"[14] "A wish! A wish! / O lovely chink, O White / Way to another grace!"[15] "I want the old rage, the lash of primordial milk!"[16] "Lave me, ultimate waters";[17] "I longed to be that thing, / The pure sensuous form."[18] An inability or an unwillingness to participate in the act of wishing can be a formidable barrier in responding to Roethke.

That Roethke's yearning is deliberate—perhaps, too, an implicit recognition of the difficulty of evoking his reader's response to his purpose, or of being a poet in the romantic tradition—is confirmed by this passage

---

[11] The first six poems in *The Far Field* (1964).   [12] "Prayer."   [13] "Epidermal Macabre."   [14] "Last Words."   [15] "O Lull Me, Lull Me."   [16] "The Lost Son."   [17] "Praise to the End."   [18] "Snake."

from the first poem of the "North American Sequence," "The Longing," in which he defines the problem to which the sequence attempts to provide a resolution:

I would with the fish, the blackening salmon, and the mad lemmings,
The children dancing, the flowers widening.
Who sighs from far away?
I would unlearn the lingo of exasperation, all the distortions of malice
and hatred;
I would believe my pain: and the eye quiet on the growing rose;
I would delight in my hands, the branch singing, altering the excessive bird;

(There follows what seems to be the central statement of his wish:)

I long for the imperishable quiet at the heart of form;

What is Roethke doing here to engage us whether we are willing to be engaged or not? Clearly the lines that precede the central statement of his wish must make his wish believable, that is, must tell us the sense in which it is believable.

We are led to notice that he is dealing with a contrast of extremes. If we are to believe that he longs for an imperishable quiet, then such quiet must be reconciled with what is not so quiet at all, such as mad lemmings, children dancing, and the branch singing, and it must also be related to his focus on growth, particularly the flowers widening and the variant growing rose. His structure is essentially one of cause and effect or of means in relation to ends; that is, because of his experience of sound and movement (cause or means), he is led to want the opposite, but in the sense that the opposite, quiet and no movement, is an arresting, a making permanent, of the life experience which he cherishes. He is close to the paradoxes of noiseless noise and still movement, and indeed his phrase, "imperishable quiet," placed as it is placed, comprehends such paradox. Similarly, the growth motif, while suggesting that what grows must perish, also suggests the imperishable.

Another way to state the paradox is that Roethke wants to be both in life and out of it at the same time. We recall Yeats in "Sailing to Byzantium" longing to be gathered "Into the artifice of eternity," but Roethke's emphasis is not that he is "fastened to a dying animal," but rather such sense experiences as "delight in my hands," a phrase which rather than being merely surface rhetoric comes to have an interior because it participates in a larger and a controlled structure. In other words, each such phrase becomes a metaphor or a symbol which both contributes to a whole pattern and at the same time draws its own meaning from that pattern. Roethke thus finds many objective correlatives for his particular state of feeling and thus creates the total effect of an original style.

Although some readers might have unlimited resistance to participation in Roethke's wish or longing, it should be clear from our view of this passage in "The Longing" that his power to dramatize the quality of his experience is formidable. But we are not surprised that he sometimes puts too great a burden on wishing and thus complicates the already difficult problem of engaging the modern reader who may be reluctant to participate in what might seem, however permanent and universal, to be only worn romanticism or idealism. In other words, although Roethke is highly aware of the poem as a dramatic structure with certain expectations that need to be met, he does not always fulfill these expectations. M. L. Rosenthal comments to this effect while examining "The Shape of the Fire," in which he sees Roethke's attempt to transcend—that is, to realize the feeling of transcendence in a poem—concluding in a weak wish:

. . . he tries to conceptualize and to give his poems a further implication of victory over the frenzy through a Freudian rebirth of the Self. These efforts are not, by and large, very convincing. Thus, the last two movements of "The Shape of the Fire" are attempts to soar and transcend in the old sense—like the ending of "Lycidas": "Tomorrow to fresh woods, and pastures new." But Milton had a vision of "the blest kingdoms meek of joy and love," while Roethke simply tells us all will be well on his own wishful authority.

—The Modern Poets (New York, 1960), p. 243

Rosenthal is perhaps severe, and it is hard to think of the quiet statement that concludes "Lycidas" as soaring, but the general criticism nevertheless has to be reckoned with. Consider, for example, the rather Wordsworthian last lines of Roethke's "The Far Field," title poem of his 1964 volume. The question is whether or not the last two lines are too wishful to carry the burden of ending a stanza, not to mention a long poem:

All finite things reveal infinitude:
The mountain with its singular bright shade
Like the blue shine on freshly frozen snow,
The after-light upon ice-burdened pines;
Odor of basswood on a mountain-slope,
A scent beloved of bees;
Silence of water above a sunken tree:
The pure serene of memory in one man,—
A ripple widening from a single stone
Winding around the waters of the world.

This is a happy ending which may be characterized, as Rosenthal characterizes the ending of "The Lost Son," as "too pat and wishful." It is not that as an ending it is so bad; rather, it is not good enough, is not a transmutation of Wordsworth into an indisputably original Roethke.

Consider by contrast the ending of "Journey to the Interior," the poem that precedes "The Far Field" in "North American Sequence":

As a blind man, lifting a curtain, knows it is morning,
I know this change:
On one side of silence there is no smile;
But when I breathe with the birds,
The spirit of wrath becomes the spirit of blessing,
And the dead begin from their dark to sing in my sleep.

Although the lines must finally be responded to in terms of the poem as a whole, they are wishful without being pat; Roethke wisely presents us with a factual statement about his personal experience and thus tends to fuse fact and wish. A line such as "The spirit of wrath becomes the spirit of blessing," which might drift in the direction of empty rhetoric, is controlled by its context.

But of course there are other reasons for the success of the stanza. Consider, for example, the relationship between the blind man in his darkness and the dead in their darkness, or the relationship between morning and singing, or the suggestive contrast that persistently controls the stanza, such as dark and light, waking and sleeping, silence and song, wrath and blessing, death and life. Consider also the unstrained devices of sound such as the *b* and *s* and then, in the last line, the *d* alliteration. The alliteration of the phrase "freshly frozen snow" in "The Far Field" seems clumsy by contrast, and the *w* alliteration of "Winding around the waters of the world" less delicate than the last line of "Journey to the Interior."

We are in effect suggesting some of the things that raise Roethke above the poet who is merely romantic. A poem such as "The Minimal" will suggest a key characteristic of his work in further answer to the question of such differentiation:

I study the lives on a leaf: the little
Sleepers, numb nudgers in cold dimensions,
Beetles in caves, newts, stone-deaf fishes,
Lice tethered to long limp subterranean weeds,
Squirmers in bogs,
And bacterial creepers
Wriggling through wounds
Like elvers in ponds,
Their wan mouths kissing the warm sutures,
Cleaning and caressing,
Creeping and healing.

The acuteness of Roethke's powers of observation is here distinct. His childhood around his father's greenhouse seems to have paid him a large dividend, as he himself was appreciatively aware, even to the point of calling the greenhouse "my symbol of the whole of life."[19] We need only ask the obvious questions—Are such powers of keen observation typical of his work from beginning to end? Are they a key aspect of his originality or his style?—and the answer to each is an obvious yes, a

[19]"Open Letter," *Mid-Century American Poets,* ed. John Ciardi (New York, 1950), p. 69. Reprinted in *On the Poet and His Craft: Selected Prose of Theodore Roethke,* ed. Ralph B. Mills, Jr. (Seattle and London, 1965), pp. 36–43.

fact which in itself would be enough to give Roethke a permanent, though minor, place in American poetry.

But not surprisingly, his aim was much larger than merely to describe. In his own words it was "a struggle for spiritual identity," "a kind of struggle out of the slime," "a history of the psyche (or allegorical journey)." "To begin from the depths and come out— that is difficult; for few know where the depths are or can recognize them; or, if they do, are afraid." Or he rephrases the same idea with humor: ". . . let's say you fish, patiently, in that dark pond, the unconscious, or dive in, with or without pants on, to come up festooned with dead cats, weeds, tin cans, and other fascinating debris. . . ."[20] His larger aim was, we would say, psychological and philosophical. Add to this the fact that ironic humor is typical of his work, and it is hard to deny (and inviting to affirm) the premise that his achievement displays the virtues of intellectual depth and complexity, plus stylistic originality.

To suggest that Roethke's achievement can be justly described in these various honorific terms is to suggest that, like any good poet, he is many poets in one. He is an acute observer, particularly of nature (things of the greenhouse and of the green world), a nature poet, as romantic poets often are. We may take "The Minimal"—or any of his "Greenhouse Poems"—as representative of his powers of observation that transcend the merely descriptive aspect of his achievement. Read "The Minimal," for example, as an erotic analogy that plays off the poet's quiet descriptive manner against a powerful content, the warmly erotic content of, for example, the climactically placed "Their wan mouths kissing the warm sutures." Or consider the last two lines of "The Minimal" in terms of dramatic structure, the lines serving to suggest aftermath or resolution and, simultaneously, sexual beginnings. Yet such a poem as "The Minimal" never loses its focus on nature.

It is, then, interesting to observe that Roethke is equally at ease in poems with other foci; for example, this stanza from his delightful nonsense poem on individuality, "The Kitty-Cat Bird":

You mew like a Cat, you grate like a Jay:
You squeak like a Mouse that's lost in the Hay,
I wouldn't be You for even a day,
—Said the Wren to the Kitty-Cat Bird.

[20]"Open Letter," passim. See also "On 'Identity,' " in On the Poet and His Craft, pp. 18–27.

How many of us would say "grate" like a jay, and with such ease—the ease of the *a* sound change from *cat* to *grate*? Or consider the ease with which Roethke in the first line balances *mew* with *grate*, *Cat* with *Jay*, or the ease with which he makes a triple rhyme sound conversational.

We may move from nonsense poem to meditation and yet see a steady Roethke. Consider this passage (in which one may hear an echo of Eliot's "Prufrock") from one of his "Meditations of an Old Woman":

Is it enough?—
The sun loosening the frost on December windows,
The glitter of wet in the first of morning?
The sound of voices, young voices, mixed with sleighbells,
Coming across snow in early evening?

Outside, the same sparrows bicker in the eaves.
I'm tired of tiny noises:
The April cheeping, the vireo's insistence,
The prattle of the young no longer pleases.
Behind the child's archness
Lurks the bad animal.

—"I'm Here"

The old woman speaks without strain, yet her observation is acute—the "sun loosening the frost," the "glitter of wet," the voices "mixed with sleighbells"—and without strain she combines sight and sound in the idea of voices "Coming across snow in early evening," all in the frame of her question, "Is it enough?" In the second stanza, again without strain, the tiny noises appear in a progression, *cheeping, insistence, prattle,* with the matter-of-factness of the old woman's statement, "The prattle of the young no longer pleases," played off against the implication that her anger is mounting, an implication confirmed in the grimness of her final statement, which, though a controlled assertion, is like an outburst of despair. From nature poem to nonsense poem to meditation, then, and yet a steady Roethke.

If reluctantly we apply the hackneyed classification "nature poet" to Roethke, we would have to show equal reluctance in asking whether or not he is in his main achievement a "love poet," which he is. Look in nearly every anthology of American poetry that includes the twentieth century—and in many general poetry anthologies—and you will find a Roethke poem called "I Knew a Woman," one of the most famous poems of our time:

I knew a woman, lovely in her bones,
When small birds sighed, she would sigh back at them;
Ah, when she moved, she moved more ways than one:
The shapes a bright container can contain!
Of her choice virtues only gods should speak,
Or English poets who grew up on Greek
(I'd have them sing in chorus, cheek to cheek).

How well her wishes went! She stroked my chin,
She taught me Turn, and Counter-turn, and Stand;
She taught me Touch, that undulant white skin;
I nibbled meekly from her proffered hand;
She was the sickle; I, poor I, the rake,
Coming behind her for her pretty sake
(But what prodigious mowing we did make).

Love likes a gander, and adores a goose:
Her full lips pursed, the errant note to seize;
She played it quick, she played it light and loose;
My eyes, they dazzled at her flowing knees;
Her several parts could keep a pure repose,
Or one hip quiver with a mobile nose
(She moved in circles, and those circles moved).

Let seed be grass, and grass turn into hay:
I'm martyr to a motion not my own;
What's freedom for? To know eternity.
I swear she cast a shadow white as stone.
But who would count eternity in days?
These old bones live to learn her wanton ways:
(I measure time by how a body sways).

Why does everyone seem to like this poem, to accept it as a fine love poem? In general terms we respond to its energy and humor, to its affirmation of life, but more particularly we respond to its affirmation as it exemplifies style as meaning. Consider the pleasure we feel in the exuberance of the speaker, as that exuberance is controlled through rhyme and slant rhyme in Roethke's stanza, both in the opening quatrain and in the succeeding triplet. Consider also the close relationship of the rhymed triplet to the humor of the speaker: in the first stanza the plainly facetious rhyme of *speak, Greek,* and *cheek;* in the second stanza, the emphatic rhyming of *rake, sake,* and *make,* in assonance with *speak, Greek,* and *cheek,* so that the exuberant humor of the speaker is compounded through sound from the first stanza to the second; in the third stanza, the anticlimactic rhyming of *nose* with *repose;* in the last stanza, the reinforcing through sound of the strong contrast of *days* with *ways* and then the totally unexpected, and yet in a sense expected, *sways,* with the speaker thus yoking the allegedly great, eternity and time, with the sheer fact of our mortality—a body sways and ironically serves to measure both the speaker's mortality and its own—thus yoking and thus wringing for us a victory of mortality over time. The speaker has modulated his tone with care from the gusty and facetious humor of the first stanza to the mature affirmation, based upon knowing a woman—inevitably in the Biblical sense of a sexual knowing—of the last.

Since "I Knew a Woman" is a fine love poem (an adaptation of the classical pastoral) and a Roethke poem too, we are not surprised to find that it shows the poet's acute power of observation, his ability to describe. In the first two stanzas this observation strongly, but not exclusively, takes the form of metaphor. "The shapes a bright container can contain!" The exclamation is perfect in context and perfect Roethke—accurate, humorous, original, particularly in the wryly witty use of the verb *contain* following the noun *container,* though *contain* in the sense of "keep within proper bounds" is a deliberate ironic contrast rather than the kind of apparent similarity represented by the repetition. In "She was the sickle; I, poor I, the rake," Roethke has moved from a concentration upon her to their mutual engagement. Considering that his woman cannot be kept within bounds, his erotic metaphor is perfectly appropriate, particularly in the hilarity of the pun on rake (garden implement and profligate) and in the mock-weary "I, poor I." Roethke also presents the exaggeration of "prodigious mowing" in a matter-of-fact way and thus secures a humor of understatement in accord with the speaker's character—a thoughtful man, aware of "These old bones."

In the third and fourth stanzas Roethke's observation, though in a pastoral frame of reference, becomes literal. The hilarity of the pun on rake is continued, yet toned down, in the first line of the third stanza, "Love likes a gander, and adores a goose." The puns on the figurative and slang senses of *gander*, "a foolish fellow" (such as, ironically, the speaker himself) and a "look" or "glance," and of *goose*, "a silly person" (his woman) and "a sudden and playful prod on the backside," are perhaps more subtle, more slyly vulgar than the pun on *rake*. Or consider as an example of the imaginative appeal of the literal, "Or one hip quiver with a mobile nose." Not many before Roethke combine an observation of a hip and a nose like this. Consider also his statement of the paradox, "She moved in circles, and those circles moved." The paradox is presented not as abstract speculation but as an observation. As a lover with a touch of the profligate in him, the speaker appropriately keeps his eyes on his woman. In the last stanza paradox appears again as observation, "I swear she cast a shadow white as stone," as if the speaker is both imagining love and experiencing a mild hallucination because of it. His acute powers of observation apply both to his physical surroundings and to what might be called his psychological surroundings. Though for want of better phrases we must say that Roethke is a "nature poet" and a "love poet," our real emphasis comes to be the depth or the quality of his experience as it is comprehended in his poems.

It is clear from "The Minimal" and from "I Knew a Woman" that as a love poet Roethke is often distinctly an erotic poet, but he achieves stature as an erotic poet because he has serious purpose (and this despite the fact that he readily stoops to the sensational). To confirm his achievement as an erotic love poet, turn to such poems as "Give Way, Ye Gates," "O Thou Opening, O," and "Slug." Or consider the lovely and but mildly erotic opening of "The Dream," viewing it, perhaps, as a tonal contrast to "I Knew a Woman":

I met her as a blossom on a stem
Before she ever breathed, and in that dream
The mind remembers from a deeper sleep:
Eye learned from eye, cold lip from sensual lip.
My dream divided on a point of fire;
Light hardened on the water where we were;
A bird sang low; the moonlight sifted in;
The water rippled, and she rippled on.

Masculine rhyme gives way to slant rhyme, and the exaggerations and the wit of "I Knew a Woman" are muted. And yet "prodigious mowing" and "she rippled on," though radically different in tone, are alike in their questing after the qualities of an experience.

To the characterization of Roethke as a nature poet and a love poet, we can surely add that he is a philosophical poet; but I think the more appropriate term to apply is *meditative*, thus making him at once nature poet, love poet, and meditative poet, persistently observing, persistently in one sense or another loving, persistently thinking about the condition of being human. He is a meditative poet because he *chooses* to meditate, as in his five "Meditations of an Old Woman" and, more largely, as a matter of his temperament. He is also a meditative poet in a way that would connect him with a tradition of religious meditation as outlined, for example, in two studies by Louis Martz, *The Poetry of Meditation* (New Haven, Connecticut, 1954) and *The Paradise Within* (New Haven, Connecticut, 1964). In the latter, works by Vaughan, Traherne, and Milton are approached "from the standpoint of the Augustinian concept of interior 'illumination,'" which involves a way of carrying on an inquiry "into the incomprehensible" (Preface, vii, xix). One of Roethke's most persistent metaphors is that of light, and his longing "for the imperishable quiet at the heart of form" is clearly a longing for a beatific vision. The phrase, in fact, links him in the twentieth century to the T. S. Eliot of *Four Quartets*—"heart of light," "the still point of the turning world," "the light is still / At the still point of the turning world";[21] "The point of intersection of the timeless / With time";[22] "A condition of complete simplicity."[23] As for the inquiry into the incomprehensible, we recall Roethke's concern for "the depths," for knowing where they are, and for recognizing them. In his "North American Sequence" he attempts his "allegorical journey."

Although a brief introduction to Roethke's achievement is not the place for an analysis of the long "North American Sequence," we may conclude with some observations on the Sequence as a whole and with a close look at its last poem, "The Rose," in order to show Roethke—in action, as it were—as a meditative poet, and thus to complete our suggestion that his achievement is original, complex, and deep and also that it presents us with a poet recognizable as nature poet, love poet, and meditative poet, usually all three at once.

---

[21]"Burnt Norton."   [22]"Dry Salvages."   [23]"Little Gidding."

In structure, the "North American Sequence" is dramatically conceived. The movement is *toward* some kind of peace or reconciliation, "the imperishable quiet at the heart of form." The movement is *from* "this sensual emptiness," which is presented as an image of horror in the opening lines of "The Longing":

On things asleep, no balm:
A kingdom of stinks and sighs,
Fetor of cockroaches, dead fish, petroleum,
Worse than castoreum of mink or weasels,
Saliva dripping from warm microphones,
Agony of crucifixion on barstools.
    Less and less the illuminated lips,
    Hands active, eyes cherished;
    Happiness left to dogs and children—

These lines have the Roethke power. They define the problem by making us see and feel it. Particularly effective is Roethke's device of playing off the casual, reflective mood of the speaker against the shock of what he is saying, a shock climaxed by the brilliant placement of "Saliva dripping from warm microphones," which presents man and his ways as part of the kingdom from which up to that moment he had been flatteringly excluded. But once included, man becomes the center of the scene, and we are left to reflect upon the contrast—and, ironically, upon the comparison—between Christ on the cross and modern man on a barstool.

In the Sequence the movement between "this sensual emptiness" and "the imperishable quiet at the heart of form" is essentially a "long journey out of the self," with focus upon experiences which the speaker finds meaningful as he reflects upon his life, past and present. He thus recalls, for example, the early days of the automobile in this Whitmanlike passage:

I remember how it was to drive in gravel,
Watching for dangerous down-hill places, where the wheels whined
                                 beyond eighty—

When you hit the deep pit at the bottom of the swale,
The trick was to throw the car sideways and charge over the hill, full of
                                                                    the throttle.
Grinding up and over the narrow road, spitting and roaring.
A chance? Perhaps. But the road was part of me, and its ditches,
And the dust lay thick on my eyelids,—Who ever wore goggles?—
                                                    —"Journey to the Interior"

Such a passage, in itself, does not take the speaker very far in the "long
journey out of the self," nor is it intended to. Roethke is at pains to
avoid a fatuous analogy. He moves with the mind, sometimes suggesting
his location in time and place with such detail as "to drive on gravel,"
or "goggles," other times creating the specific vagueness of such lines
as these (an Eliot echo):

In the moment of time when the small drop forms, but does not fall,
I have known the heart of the sun,—
In the dark and light of a dry place,
In a flicker of fire brisked by a dusty wind.
I have heard, in a drip of leaves,
A slight song,
After the midnight cries.

                                                    —"Journey to the Interior"

The effect of both techniques is to place us in a mind moving mainly by
association in an unhurried progress to the end of its journey. This end is
just the one Roethke states at the outset—in a meditation it is perfectly
appropriate to perceive at the outset the conclusion that will be reached.

Since the character of the meditation is such that there is no attempt,
no desire, to hold as a dramatic revelation the answer to the question of
what conclusion will be reached, the whole emphasis becomes whether
or not the poet can make us feel the reality of the conclusion he reaches.
It is a supreme challenge for any poet, and particularly for a poet who
would be accused—and rightly so if he failed—of using threadbare
literary formulas rather than truly exploring the meaning of his experience. But Roethke meets the challenge in "The Rose."

"The Rose" is a poem of 114 lines in four parts roughly equal in length. Quantitatively the poem is nearly all description either of the actual place where the speaker stands or of his past experience. Although Roethke makes no effort to hold back assertion about, or judgment of, the meaning of his experience, he places assertion or judgment with great care. The question is, of course, How does he combine description and assertion into a poem of mood, into a religious meditation? The opening stanza provides a clue:

There are those to whom place is unimportant,
But this place, where sea and fresh water meet,
Is important—
Where the hawks sway out into the wind,
Without a single wingbeat,
And the eagles sail low over the fir trees,
And the gulls cry against the crows
In the curved harbors,
And the tide rises up against the grass
Nibbled by sheep and rabbits.

Rather than being undramatic, the quiet opening statement is actually cast in dramatic images through which the speaker asserts his values. It is as if he consciously challenges himself to make us (and himself) feel the reality of the importance of place. Thus, in the lines following the opening statement, he reveals his control over what he is doing by telling us what the place is like, rather than by explaining its importance. The second stanza continues the description of place but significantly ends with a statement that functions in two ways: "And there is silence." Roethke means this literally, the immediate reference being "the cries of the owl, the eerie whooper." But the statement also suggests the speaker's feeling for the larger question of the relation of sound to silence, man in a universe of silence, which in turn suggests an ultimate silence, in a positive sense a union with God.

Roethke's control is brilliantly confirmed by the opening of Part III: "What do they tell us, sound and silence?"; as with the opening of Part I, rather than stating what sound and silence tell us, he refers at once to "American sounds in this silence" and then describes the American sounds. For example:

The bobolink skirring from a broken fencepost,
The bluebird, lover of holes in old wood, lilting its light song,
And that thin cry, like a needle piercing the ear, the insistent cicada,
And the ticking of snow around oil drums in the Dakotas,
The thin whine of telephone wires in the wind of a Michigan winter,
The shriek of nails as old shingles are ripped from the top of a roof,
The bulldozer backing away, the hiss of the sandblaster,
And the deep chorus of horns coming up from the streets in early morning.

The third stanza of Part I switches to the first-person point of view, a switch which reinforces the philosophical broadening suggested by "And there is silence":

I sway outside myself
Into the darkening currents,

Soon the speaker asks a question which concludes Part I, but the question is also a mild incantation:

Was it here I wore a crown of birds for a moment
While on a far point of the rocks
The light heightened,
And below, in a mist out of nowhere,
The first rain gathered?

A "crown of birds" recalls, by contrast, a crown of thorns. The speaker is aware—makes us aware—of the symbolic nature of his experience.

Having established his religious-philosophical or meditative mood and the symbolic character of his experience, Roethke could do nothing more appropriate than to concentrate on the symbolic meaning of his experience. This he does, but he makes us feel the reality of his experience in his choice of a focal symbol. It is, of all things, the rose—and again we are back to Eliot, who went back to Dante. Roethke's rose, however, is very much his own; it is the "rose in the sea-wind." All preceding description functions to dramatize its appearance, and significantly the incantatory mood of the speaker is maintained (note the use of repetition):

But this rose, this rose in the sea-wind,
Stays,
Stays in its true place,
Flowering out of the dark,
Widening at high noon, face upward,
A single wild rose, struggling out of the white embrace of the morning-
glory,
Out of the briary hedge, the tangle of matted underbrush,
Beyond the clover, the ragged hay,
Beyond the sea pine, the oak, the wind-tipped madrona,
Moving with the waves, the undulating driftwood,
Where the slow creek winds down to the black sand of the shore
With its thick grassy scum and crabs scuttling back into their glistening
craters.

The end of Part II is a recollection of the poet's youthful experience in the greenhouse, also a place of roses; past and present are united. Part II concludes with a reference to his father: "What need for heaven, then, / With that man, and those roses?" But the need for heaven, it will turn out, is acute.

By the end of Part II Roethke's description is functioning as a glimpse of heaven on earth, though the heaven is what is, including "the hiss of the sandblaster," rather than a sentimentalizing of what is. Following his description of American sounds in Part III, he affirms the heaven within:

I return to the twittering of swallows above water,
And that sound, that single sound,
When the mind remembers all,
And gently the light enters the sleeping soul,
A sound so thin it could not woo a bird,

Beautiful my desire, and the place of my desire.

But in Part IV he must, while affirming, conclude his meditation dramatically. The poem inevitably returns to the rose in the sea-wind and makes it a climactic symbol, a suggestion of a glimpse of heaven, the speaker's vision.

Here is the ending of "The Rose," combining the symbols of the rose and of light, in its way soaring:

And I rejoiced in being what I was:
In the lilac change, the white reptilian calm,
In the bird beyond the bough, the single one
With all the air to greet him as he flies,
The dolphin rising from the darkening waves;

And in this rose, this rose in the sea-wind,
Rooted in stone, keeping the whole of light,
Gathering to itself sound and silence—
Mine and the sea-wind's.

These are lines we feel and believe as poetry. The meditation ends in the vision sought from the beginning. At the end of the poem we know why "this place, where sea and fresh water meet, / Is important."

So Roethke is, as the dust jacket—not the place where one ordinarily seeks accurate critical judgments—of his last book proclaims him, "a major American poet." Although he invites comparison with poets in the romantic tradition—in the larger tradition of nature poetry and of love poetry, and in the American tradition with the rhythms and energy of Whitman—and with the poets in the tradition of religious meditation, particularly with Eliot—the rose, and light, and form—it is, of course, singularly inappropriate to rate him, or any poet, on a scale, such as in relation to Eliot or Yeats. "Major American poet" describes Theodore Roethke well enough because he succeeds in doing what a major poet has to do—he teaches us how to feel.

William J. Martz

A NOTE ON THE SELECTION

The following selection of Roethke's poems is in the chronological order of their publication in collections except for the opening selection from *I Am! Says the Lamb* (1961): the poems "Vernal Sentiment," "Snake," "Root Cellar," "Orchids," and "Frau Bauman, Frau Schmidt, and Frau Schwartze" appear also in *Words for the Wind* (1958). "Vernal Sentiment," in turn, is from *Open House* (1941) and if strict chronological order were followed, would precede "Night Journey" in the present selection. "Snake" is a new poem in *Words for the Wind* and would chronologically precede "Slug" in the present selection. The other three are from *The Lost Son* (1948) and would precede "Dolor" in the present selection. The decision to open with "The Nonsense Poems" and "The Greenhouse Poems" is based upon the appropriateness of the groupings as an introduction to Roethke.

THE KITTY-CAT BIRD

The Kitty-Cat Bird, he sat on a Fence.
Said the Wren, your Song isn't worth 10¢.
You're a Fake, you're a Fraud, you're a Hor-rid Pretense!
    —Said the Wren to the Kitty-Cat Bird.

5 You've too many Tunes, and none of them Good:
I wish you would act like a bird really should,
Or stay by yourself down deep in the wood,
    —Said the Wren to the Kitty-Cat Bird.

You mew like a Cat, you grate like a Jay:
10 You squeak like a Mouse that's lost in the Hay,
I wouldn't be You for even a day,
    —Said the Wren to the Kitty-Cat Bird.

The Kitty-Cat Bird, he moped and he cried.
Then a real cat came with a Mouth so Wide,
15 That the Kitty-Cat Bird just hopped inside;
"At last I'm myself!"—and he up and died
    —Did the Kitty—the Kitty-Cat Bird.

You'd better not laugh; and don't say, "Pooh!"
Until you have thought this Sad Tale through:
20 Be sure that whatever you are is you
    —Or you'll end like the Kitty-Cat Bird.

THE CHAIR

A funny thing about a Chair:
You hardly ever think it's *there*.
To know a Chair is really it,
You sometimes have to go and sit.

THE SLOTH

In moving-slow he has no Peer.
You ask him something in his ear;
He thinks about it for a Year;

And, then, before he says a Word
5 There, upside down (unlike a Bird)
He will assume that you have Heard—

A most Ex-as-per-at-ing Lug.
But should you call his manner Smug,
He'll sigh and give his Branch a Hug;

10 Then off again to Sleep he goes,
Still swaying gently by his Toes,
And you just *know* he knows he knows.

THE BOY AND THE BUSH

A Boy who had Gumption and Push
Would frequently Talk to a Bush,
And the Bush would say, "Mac,
I'd like to Talk Back,
5 If I thought you could Hear in a Hush."

Now Nobody Sniggered and Mocked
As Those Two quietly Talked,
Because Nobody Heard,
Not a Beast, Not a Bird,—
10 So they Talked and they Talked and they Talked.

22

VERNAL SENTIMENT

Though the crocuses poke up their heads in the usual places,
The frog scum appear on the pond with the same froth of green,
And boys moon at girls with last year's fatuous faces,
I never am bored, however familiar the scene.

5 When from under the barn the cat brings a similar litter,—
Two yellow and black, and one that looks in between,—
Though it all happened before, I cannot grow bitter:
I rejoice in the spring, as though no spring ever had been.

SNAKE

I saw a young snake glide
Out of the mottled shade
And hang, limp on a stone:
A thin mouth, and a tongue
5 Stayed, in the still air.

It turned; it drew away;
Its shadow bent in half;
It quickened, and was gone.

I felt my slow blood warm.
10 I longed to be that thing,
The pure, sensuous form.
And I may be, some time.

ROOT CELLAR

Nothing would sleep in that cellar, dank as a ditch,
Bulbs broke out of boxes hunting for chinks in the dark,
Shoots dangled and drooped,
Lolling obscenely from mildewed crates,
5 Hung down long yellow evil necks, like tropical snakes.
And what a congress of stinks!—
Roots ripe as old bait,
Pulpy stems, rank, silo-rich,
Leaf-mold, manure, lime, piled against slippery planks.
10 Nothing would give up life:
Even the dirt kept breathing a small breath.

ORCHIDS

They lean over the path,
Adder-mouthed,
Swaying close to the face,
Coming out, soft and deceptive,
5 Limp and damp, delicate as a young bird's tongue;
Their fluttery fledgling lips
Move slowly,
Drawing in the warm air.

And at night,
10 The faint moon falling through whitewashed glass,
The heat going down
So their musky smell comes even stronger,
Drifting down from their mossy cradles:
So many devouring infants!
15 Soft luminescent fingers,
Lips neither dead nor alive,
Loose ghostly mouths
Breathing.

FRAU BAUMAN, FRAU SCHMIDT,
AND FRAU SCHWARTZE

Gone the three ancient ladies
Who creaked on the greenhouse ladders,
Reaching up white strings
To wind, to wind
5 The sweet-pea tendrils, the smilax,
Nasturtiums, the climbing
Roses, to straighten
Carnations, red
Chrysanthemums; the stiff
10 Stems, jointed like corn,
They tied and tucked,—
These nurses of nobody else.
Quicker than birds, they dipped
Up and sifted the dirt;
15 They sprinkled and shook;
They stood astride pipes,
Their skirts billowing out wide into tents,
Their hands twinkling with wet;
Like witches they flew along rows
20 Keeping creation at ease;
With a tendril for needle
They sewed up the air with a stem;
They teased out the seed that the cold kept asleep,—
All the coils, loops, and whorls.
25 They trellised the sun; they plotted for more than themselves.

I remember how they picked me up, a spindly kid,
Pinching and poking my thin ribs
Till I lay in their laps, laughing,
Weak as a whiffet;
30 Now, when I'm alone and cold in my bed,
They still hover over me,
These ancient leathery crones,
With their bandannas stiffened with sweat,
And their thorn-bitten wrists,
35 And their snuff-laden breath blowing lightly over me in my first sleep.

OPEN HOUSE

My secrets cry aloud.
I have no need for tongue.
My heart keeps open house,
My doors are widely swung.
5 An epic of the eyes
My love, with no disguise.

My truths are all foreknown,
This anguish self-revealed.
I'm naked to the bone,
10 With nakedness my shield.
Myself is what I wear:
I keep the spirit spare.

The anger will endure,
The deed will speak the truth
15 In language strict and pure.
I stop the lying mouth:
Rage warps my clearest cry
To witless agony.

PRAYER

If I must of my Senses lose,
I pray Thee, Lord, that I may choose
Which of the Five I shall retain
Before oblivion clouds the brain.
5 My Tongue is generations dead,
My Nose defiles a comely head;
For hearkening to carnal evils
My Ears have been the very devil's.

And some have held the Eye to be
10 The instrument of lechery,
More furtive than the Hand in low
And vicious venery—Not so!
Its rape is gentle, never more
Violent than a metaphor.
15 In truth, the Eye's the abettor of
The holiest platonic love:
Lip, Breast and Thigh cannot possess
So singular a blessedness.
Therefore, O Lord, let me preserve
20 The Sense that does so fitly serve,
Take Tongue and Ear—all else I have—
Let Light attend me to the grave!

EPIDERMAL MACABRE

Indelicate is he who loathes
The aspect of his fleshy clothes,—
The flying fabric stitched on bone,
The vesture of the skeleton,
5 The garment neither fur nor hair,
The cloak of evil and despair,
The veil long violated by
Caresses of the hand and eye.
Yet such is my unseemliness:
10 I hate my epidermal dress,
The savage blood's obscenity,
The rags of my anatomy,
And willingly would I dispense
With false accouterments of sense,
15 To sleep immodestly, a most
Incarnadine and carnal ghost.

NIGHT JOURNEY

Now as the train bears west,
Its rhythm rocks the earth,
And from my Pullman berth
I stare into the night
5 While others take their rest.
Bridges of iron lace,
A suddenness of trees,
A lap of mountain mist
All cross my line of sight,
10 Then a bleak wasted place,
And a lake below my knees.
Full on my neck I feel
The straining at a curve;
My muscles move with steel,
15 I wake in every nerve.
I watch a beacon swing
From dark to blazing bright;
We thunder through ravines
And gullies washed with light.
20 Beyond the mountain pass
Mist deepens on the pane;
We rush into a rain
That rattles double glass.
Wheels shake the roadbed stone,
25 The pistons jerk and shove,
I stay up half the night
To see the land I love.

DOLOR

I have known the inexorable sadness of pencils,
Neat in their boxes, dolor of pad and paper-weight,
All the misery of manilla folders and mucilage,
Desolation in immaculate public places,
5 Lonely reception room, lavatory, switchboard,
The unalterable pathos of basin and pitcher,
Ritual of multigraph, paper-clip, comma,
Endless duplication of lives and objects.
And I have seen dust from the walls of institutions,
10 Finer than flour, alive, more dangerous than silica,
Sift, almost invisible, through long afternoons of tedium,
Dropping a fine film on nails and delicate eyebrows,
Glazing the pale hair, the duplicate gray standard faces.

NIGHT CROW

When I saw that clumsy crow
Flap from a wasted tree,
A shape in the mind rose up:
Over the gulfs of dream
5 Flew a tremendous bird
Further and further away
Into a moonless black,
Deep in the brain, far back.

BRING THE DAY!

1

Bees and lilies there were,
Bees and lilies there were,
Either to other,—
Which would you rather?
5   Bees and lilies were there.

The green grasses,—would they?
The green grasses?—
She asked her skin
To let me in:
10   The far leaves were for it.

Forever is easy, she said.
How many angels do you know?—
And over by Algy's
Something came by me,
15 It wasn't a goose,
It wasn't a poodle.

Everything's closer. Is this a cage?
The chill's gone from the moon.
Only the woods are alive.
20 I can't marry the dirt.

I'm a biscuit. I'm melted already.
The white weather hates me.
Why is how I like it.
I can't catch a bush.

2

25 The herrings are awake.
What's all the singing between?—
Is it with whispers and kissing?—
I've listened into the least waves.
The grass says what the wind says:
30 Begin with the rock;
End with water.

When I stand, I'm almost a tree.
Leaves, do you like me any?
A swan needs a pond.
35 The worm and the rose
Both love
Rain.

3

O small bird wakening,
Light as a hand among blossoms,
40 Hardly any old angels are around any more.
The air's quiet under the small leaves.
The dust, the long dust, stays.
The spiders sail into summer.
It's time to begin!
45 To begin!

GIVE WAY, YE GATES

1

Believe me, knot of gristle, I bleed like a tree;
I dream of nothing but boards;
I could love a duck.

Such music in a skin!
5 A bird sings in the bush of your bones.
Tufty, the water's loose.
Bring me a finger. This dirt's lonesome for grass.
Are the rats dancing? The cats are.
And you, cat after great milk and vasty fishes,
10 A moon loosened from a stag's eye,
Twiced me nicely,—
In the green of my sleep,
In the green.

2

Mother of blue and the many changes of hay,
15 This tail hates a flat path.
I've let my nose out;
I could melt down a stone,—
How is it with the long birds?
May I look too, loved eye?
20 It's a wink beyond the world.
In the slow rain, who's afraid?
We're king and queen of the right ground.
I'll risk the winter for you.

You tree beginning to know,
25 You whisper of kidneys,
We'll swinge the instant!—
With jots and jogs and cinders on the floor:
The sea will be there, the great squashy shadows,
Biting themselves perhaps;
30 The shrillest frogs;
And the ghost of some great howl
Dead in a wall.

In the high-noon of thighs,
In the springtime of stones,
35 We'll stretch with the great stems.
We'll be at the business of what might be
Looking toward what we are.

3

You child with a beast's heart,
Make me a bird or a bear!
40 I've played with the fishes
Among the unwrinkling ferns
In the wake of a ship of wind;
But now the instant ages,
And my thought hunts another body.
45 I'm sad with the little owls.

4

Touch and arouse. Suck and sob. Curse and mourn.
It's a cold scrape in a low place.
The dead crow dries on a pole.
Shapes in the shade
50 Watch.

The mouth asks. The hand takes.
These wings are from the wrong nest.
Who stands in a hole
Never spills.

55 I hear the clap of an old wind.
The cold knows when to come.
What beats in me
I still bear.

The deep stream remembers:
60 Once I was a pond.
What slides away
Provides.

THE LONG ALLEY

1

A river glides out of the grass. A river or a serpent.
A fish floats belly upward,
Sliding through the white current,
Slowly turning,
5 Slowly.

The dark flows on itself. A dead mouth sings under an old tree.
The ear hears only in low places.
Remember an old sound.
Remember
10 Water.

This slag runs slow. What bleeds when metal breaks?
Flesh, you offend this metal. How long need the bones mourn?
Are those horns on top of the hill? Yesterday has a long look.

Loo, loo, said the sulphurous water,
15 There's no filth on a plateau of cinders.
This smoke's from the glory of God.

Can you name it? I can't name it.
Let's not hurry. The dead don't hurry.
Who else breathes here? What does the grave say?
20   My gates are all caves.

2

The fiend's far away. Lord, what do you require?
    The soul resides in the horse barn.
Believe me, there's no one else, kitten-limp sister.
    Kiss the trough, swine-on-Friday.
25 Come to me, milk-nose. I need a loan of the quick.
    There's no joy in soft bones.
For whom were you made, sweetness I cannot touch?
    Look what the larks do.
Luminous one, shall we meet on the bosom of God?
30   Return the gaze of a pond.

3

Stay close. Must I kill something else?
Can feathers eat me? There's no clue in the silt.
This wind gives me scales. Have mercy, gristle:
It's my last waltz with an old itch.

35   A waiting ghost warms up the dead
       Until they creak their knees:
       So up and away and what do we do
       But barley-break and squeeze.

       Tricksy comes and tricksy goes
40   Bold in fear therefore;
       The hay hops in the horse's mouth,
       The chin jumps to the nose.

       Rich me cherries a fondling's kiss,
       The summer bumps of ha:
45   Hand me a feather, I'll fan you warm,
       I'm happy with my paws.

Gilliflower ha,
Gilliflower ho,
My love's locked in
50 The old silo.
She cries to the hen,
She waves to the goose,

But they don't come
To let her loose.

55   If we detach
        The head of a match
        What do we do
        To the cat's wish?
        Do we rout the fish?
60   Will the goat's mouth
        Have the last laugh?

        4

That was a close knock. See what the will wants.
This air could flesh a dead stick. Sweet Jesus, make me sweat.
Are the flowers here? The birds are.
65 Shall I call the flowers?

        Come littlest, come tenderest,
        Come whispering over the small waters,
        Reach me rose, sweet one, still moist in the loam,
        Come, come out of the shade, the cool ways,
70   The long alleys of string and stem;
        Bend down, small breathers, creepers and winders;
        Lean from the tiers and benches,
        Cyclamen dripping and lilies.
        What fish-ways you have, littlest flowers,
75   Swaying over the walks, in the watery air,
        Drowsing in soft light, petals pulsing.

Light airs! Light airs! A pierce of angels!
The leaves, the leaves become me!
The tendrils have me!

5

80 Bricks flake before my face. Master of water, that's trees away.
Reach me a peach, fondling, the hills are there.
Nuts are money: wherefore and what else?
Send down a rush of air, O torrential,
Make the sea flash in the dust.

85 Call off the dogs, my paws are gone.
This wind brings many fish;
The lakes will be happy:
Give me my hands:
I'll take the fire.

THE SHAPE OF THE FIRE

1

What's this? A dish for fat lips.
Who says? A nameless stranger.
Is he a bird or a tree? Not everyone can tell.

Water recedes to the crying of spiders.
5 An old scow bumps over black rocks.
A cracked pod calls.

Mother me out of here. What more will the bones allow?
Will the sea give the wind suck? A toad folds into a stone.
These flowers are all fangs. Comfort me, fury.
10 Wake me, witch, we'll do the dance of rotten sticks.

Shale loosens. Marl reaches into the field. Small birds pass over water.
Spirit, come near. This is only the edge of whiteness.
I can't laugh at a procession of dogs.

In the hour of ripeness, the tree is barren.
15 The she-bear mopes under the hill.
Mother, mother, stir from your cave of sorrow.

A low mouth laps water. Weeds, weeds, how I love you.
The arbor is cooler. Farewell, farewell, fond worm.
The warm comes without sound.

2

20 Where's the eye?
The eye's in the sty.
The ear's not here
Beneath the hair.
When I took off my clothes
25 To find a nose,
There was only one shoe
For the waltz of To,
The pinch of Where.

Time for the flat-headed man. I recognize that listener,
30 Him with the platitudes and rubber doughnuts,
Melting at the knees, a varicose horror.
Hello, hello. My nerves knew you, dear boy.
Have you come to unhinge my shadow?
Last night I slept in the pits of a tongue.
35 The silver fish ran in and out of my special bindings;
I grew tired of the ritual of names and the assistant keeper of the mollusks:
Up over a viaduct I came, to the snakes and sticks of another winter,
A two-legged dog hunting a new horizon of howls.
The wind sharpened itself on a rock;
40 A voice sang:

        Pleasure on ground
        Has no sound,
        Easily maddens
        The uneasy man.

45   Who, careless, slips
        In coiling ooze
        Is trapped to the lips,
        Leaves more than shoes;

        Must pull off clothes
50   To jerk like a frog
        On belly and nose
        From the sucking bog.

My meat eats me. Who waits at the gate?
Mother of quartz, your words writhe into my ear.
55 Renew the light, lewd whisper.

    3

The wasp waits.
    The edge cannot eat the center.
The grape glistens.
    The path tells little to the serpent.
60 An eye comes out of the wave.
    The journey from flesh is longest.

A rose sways least.
   The redeemer comes a dark way.

4

Morning-fair, follow me further back
65 Into that minnowy world of weeds and ditches,
When the herons floated high over the white houses,
And the little crabs slipped into silvery craters.
When the sun for me glinted the sides of a sand grain,
And my intent stretched over the buds at their first trembling.

70 That air and shine: and the flicker's loud summer call:
The bearded boards in the stream and the all of apples;
The glad hen on the hill; and the trellis humming.
Death was not. I lived in a simple drowse:
Hands and hair moved through a dream of wakening blossoms.
75 Rain sweetened the cave and the dove still called;
The flowers leaned on themselves, the flowers in hollows;
And love, love sang toward.

5

To have the whole air!
The light, the full sun
80 Coming down on the flowerheads,
The tendrils turning slowly,
A slow snail-lifting, liquescent;
To be by the rose
Rising slowly out of its bed,
85 Still as a child in its first loneliness;
To see cyclamen veins become clearer in early sunlight,
And mist lifting out of the brown cattails;
To stare into the after-light, the glitter left on the lake's surface,
When the sun has fallen behind a wooded island;
90 To follow the drops sliding from a lifted oar,
Held up, while the rower breathes, and the small boat drifts quietly
                                            shoreward;
To know that light falls and fills, often without our knowing,
As an opaque vase fills to the brim from a quick pouring,
Fills and trembles at the edge yet does not flow over,
95 Still holding and feeding the stem of the contained flower.

O, THOU OPENING, O

1

I'll make it; but it may take me.
The rat's my phase.
My left side's tender.
Read me the stream.

5 Dazzle me, dizzy aphorist.
Fling me a precept.
I'm a draft sleeping by a stick;
I'm lost in what I have.

        The Depth calls to the Height
10   —Neither knows it.
        Those close to the Ground
            —Only stay out of the Wind.

Thrum-thrum, who can be equal to ease?
I've seen my father's face before
15 Deep in the belly of a thing to be.
The Devil isn't dead; he's just away.

Where's Ann? Where's Lou? Where's Jock-with-the-Wind?
Forgive me a minute, nymph.
I'll change the image, and my shoes.
20 A true mole wanders like a worm.

2

    And now are we to have that pelludious Jesus-shimmer over all things, the animal's candid gaze, a shade less than feathers, light's broken speech revived, a ghostly going of tame bears, a bright moon on gleaming skin, a thing you cannot say to whisper and equal a Wound?
    I'm tired of all that, Bag-Foot. I can hear small angels anytime. Who cares about the dance of dead underwear, or the sad waltz of paper bags? Who ever said God sang in your fat shape? You're not the only keeper of hay. That's a spratling's prattle. And don't be thinking you're simplicity's sweet thing, either. A leaf could drag you.

Where's the great rage of a rocking heart, the high rare true dangerous indignation? Let me persuade more slowly:

The dark has its own light.
A son has many fathers.
35 Stand by a slow stream:
Hear the sigh of what is.
Be a pleased rock
On a plain day.
Waking's
40 Kissing.
Yes.

3

You mean?—
I can leap, true to the field,
In the lily's sovereign right?
45 Be a body lighted with love,
Sad, in a singing-time?
Or happy, correct as a hat?

Oh, what a webby wonder I am!
Swaying, would you believe,
50 Like a sapling tree,
Enough to please a cloud!

This frog's had another fall.
The old stalk still has a pulse;
I've crept from a cry.
55 The holy root wags the tail of a hill;
I'm true to soup, and happy to ask:
I sing the green, and things to come,
I'm king of another condition,
So alive I could die!
60 The ground's beating like flame!
You fat unnecessary hags,
You enemies of skin,—
A dolphin's at my door!
I'm twinkling like a twig!
65 The lark's my heart!

I'm wild with news!
My fancy's white!
I am my faces,
Love.

70   *Who reads in bed*
               —Fornicates on the stove.
      An old dog
               —Should sleep on his paws.

See what the sweet harp says.
75 *Should a song break a sleep?*
The round home of a root,—
Is that the place to go?
I'm a tune dying
On harsh stone.
80 *An Eye says,*
Come.

I keep dreaming of bees.
This flesh has airy bones.
Going is knowing.
85 *I see; I seek;*
I'm near.
Be true,
Skin.

ELEGY FOR JANE

MY STUDENT, THROWN BY A HORSE

I remember the neckcurls, limp and damp as tendrils;
And her quick look, a sidelong pickerel smile;
And how, once startled into talk, the light syllables leaped for her,
And she balanced in the delight of her thought,
5 A wren, happy, tail into the wind,
Her song trembling the twigs and small branches.
The shade sang with her;
The leaves, their whispers turned to kissing;
And the mold sang in the bleached valleys under the rose.

10 Oh, when she was sad, she cast herself down into such a pure depth,
Even a father could not find her:
Scraping her cheek against straw;
Stirring the clearest water.

My sparrow, you are not here,
15 Waiting like a fern, making a spiny shadow.
The sides of wet stones cannot console me,
Nor the moss, wound with the last light.

If only I could nudge you from this sleep,
My maimed darling, my skittery pigeon.
20 Over this damp grave I speak the words of my love:
I, with no rights in this matter,
Neither father nor lover.

44

FOUR FOR SIR JOHN DAVIES

1 THE DANCE

Is that dance slowing in the mind of man
That made him think the universe could hum?
The great wheel turns its axle when it can;
I need a place to sing, and dancing-room,
5 And I have made a promise to my ears
I'll sing and whistle romping with the bears.

For they are all my friends: I saw one slide
Down a steep hillside on a cake of ice,—
Or was that in a book? I think with pride:
10 A caged bear rarely does the same thing twice
In the same way: O watch his body sway!—
This animal remembering to be gay.

I tried to fling my shadow at the moon,
The while my blood leaped with a wordless song.
15 Though dancing needs a master, I had none
To teach my toes to listen to my tongue.
But what I learned there, dancing all alone,
Was not the joyless motion of a stone.

I take this cadence from a man named Yeats;
20 I take it, and I give it back again:
For other tunes and other wanton beats
Have tossed my heart and fiddled through my brain.
Yes, I was dancing-mad, and how
That came to be the bears and Yeats would know.

2 THE PARTNER

25 Between such animal and human heat
I find myself perplexed. What is desire?—
The impulse to make someone else complete?
That woman would set sodden straw on fire.
Was I the servant of a sovereign wish,
30 Or ladle rattling in an empty dish?

We played a measure with commingled feet:
The lively dead had taught us to be fond.

Who can embrace the body of his fate?
Light altered light along the living ground.
35 She kissed me close, and then did something else.
My marrow beat as wildly as my pulse.

I'd say it to my horse: we live beyond
Our outer skin. Who's whistling up my sleeve?
I see a heron prancing in his pond;
40 I know a dance the elephants believe.
The living all assemble! What's the cue?—
Do what the clumsy partner wants to do!

Things loll and loiter. Who condones the lost?
This joy outleaps the dog. Who cares? Who cares?
45 I gave her kisses back, and woke a ghost.
O what lewd music crept into our ears!
The body and the soul know how to play
In that dark world where gods have lost their way.

3   THE WRAITH

Incomprehensible gaiety and dread
50 Attended what we did. Behind, before,
Lay all the lonely pastures of the dead;
The spirit and the flesh cried out for more.
We two, together, on a darkening day
Took arms against our own obscurity.

55 Did each become the other in that play?
She laughed me out, and then she laughed me in;
In the deep middle of ourselves we lay;
When glory failed, we danced upon a pin.
The valley rocked beneath the granite hill;
60 Our souls looked forth, and the great day stood still.

There was a body, and it cast a spell,—
God pity those but wanton to the knees,—
The flesh can make the spirit visible;
We woke to find the moonlight on our toes.

65 In the rich weather of a dappled wood
　　We played with dark and light as children should.

　　What shape leaped forward at the sensual cry?—
　　Sea-beast or bird flung toward the ravaged shore?
　　Did space shake off an angel with a sigh?
70 We rose to meet the moon, and saw no more.
　　It was and was not she, a shape alone,
　　Impaled on light, and whirling slowly down.

4   THE VIGIL

　　Dante attained the purgatorial hill,
　　Trembled at hidden virtue without flaw,
75 Shook with a mighty power beyond his will,—
　　Did Beatrice deny what Dante saw?
　　All lovers live by longing, and endure:
　　Summon a vision and declare it pure.

　　Though everything's astonishment at last,
80 Who leaps to heaven at a single bound?
　　The links were soft between us; still, we kissed;
　　We undid chaos to a curious sound:
　　The waves broke easy, cried to me in white;
　　Her look was morning in the dying light.

85 The visible obscures. But who knows when?
　　Things have their thought: they are the shards of me;
　　I thought that once, and thought comes round again;
　　Rapt, we leaned forth with what we could not see.
　　We danced to shining; mocked before the black
90 And shapeless night that made no answer back.

　　The world is for the living. Who are they?
　　We dared the dark to reach the white and warm.
　　She was the wind when wind was in my way;
　　Alive at noon, I perished in her form.
95 Who rise from flesh to spirit know the fall:
　　The word outleaps the world, and light is all.

THE WAKING

I wake to sleep, and take my waking slow.
I feel my fate in what I cannot fear.
I learn by going where I have to go.

We think by feeling. What is there to know?
5 I hear my being dance from ear to ear.
I wake to sleep, and take my waking slow.

Of those so close beside me, which are you?
God bless the Ground! I shall walk softly there,
And learn by going where I have to go.

10 Light takes the Tree; but who can tell us how?
The lowly worm climbs up a winding stair;
I wake to sleep, and take my waking slow.

Great Nature has another thing to do
To you and me; so take the lively air,
15 And, lovely, learn by going where to go.

This shaking keeps me steady. I should know.
What falls away is always. And is near.
I wake to sleep, and take my waking slow.
I learn by going where I have to go.

THE DREAM

1

I met her as a blossom on a stem
Before she ever breathed, and in that dream
The mind remembers from a deeper sleep:
Eye learned from eye, cold lip from sensual lip.
5 My dream divided on a point of fire;
  Light hardened on the water where we were;
  A bird sang low; the moonlight sifted in;
  The water rippled, and she rippled on.

2

She came toward me in the flowing air,
10 A shape of change, encircled by its fire.
  I watched her there, between me and the moon;
  The bushes and the stones danced on and on;
  I touched her shadow when the light delayed;
  I turned my face away, and yet she stayed.
15 A bird sang from the center of a tree;
  She loved the wind because the wind loved me.

3

Love is not love until love's vulnerable.
She slowed to sigh, in that long interval.
A small bird flew in circles where we stood;
20 The deer came down, out of the dappled wood.
  All who remember, doubt. Who calls that strange?
  I tossed a stone, and listened to its plunge.
  She knew the grammar of least motion, she
  Lent me one virtue, and I live thereby.

4

25 She held her body steady in the wind;
  Our shadows met, and slowly swung around;
  She turned the field into a glittering sea;
  I played in flame and water like a boy
  And I swayed out beyond the white seafoam;
30 Like a wet log, I sang within a flame.
  In that last while, eternity's confine,
  I came to love, I came into my own.

WORDS FOR THE WIND

1

Love, love, a lily's my care,
She's sweeter than a tree.
Loving, I use the air
Most lovingly: I breathe;
5 Mad in the wind I wear
Myself as I should be,
All's even with the odd,
My brother the vine is glad.

Are flower and seed the same?
10 What do the great dead say?
Sweet Phoebe, she's my theme:
She sways whenever I sway.
"O love me while I am,
You green thing in my way!"
15 I cried, and the birds came down
And made my song their own.

Motion can keep me still:
She kissed me out of thought
As a lovely substance will;
20 She wandered; I did not:
I stayed, and light fell
Across her pulsing throat;
I stared, and a garden stone
Slowly became the moon.

25 The shallow stream runs slack;
The wind creaks slowly by;
Out of a nestling's beak
Comes a tremulous cry
I cannot answer back;
30 A shape from deep in the eye—
That woman I saw in a stone—
Keeps pace when I walk alone.

2

The sun declares the earth;
The stones leap in the stream;
35 On a wide plain, beyond
The far stretch of a dream,
A field breaks like the sea;
The wind's white with her name,
And I walk with the wind.

40 The dove's my will today.
She sways, half in the sun:
Rose, easy on a stem,
One with the sighing vine,
One to be merry with,
45 And pleased to meet the moon.
She likes wherever I am.

Passion's enough to give
Shape to a random joy:
I cry delight: I know
50 The root, the core of a cry.
Swan-heart, arbutus-calm,

She moves when time is shy:
Love has a thing to do.

A fair thing grows more fair;
55 The green, the springing green
Makes an intenser day
Under the rising moon;
I smile, no mineral man;
I bear, but not alone,
60 The burden of this joy.

3
Under a southern wind,
The birds and fishes move
North, in a single stream;
The sharp stars swing around;
65 I get a step beyond
The wind, and there I am,
I'm odd and full of love.

Wisdom, where is it found?—
Those who embrace, believe.
70 Whatever was, still is,
Says a song tied to a tree.
Below, on the ferny ground,
In rivery air, at ease,
I walk with my true love.

75 What time's my heart? I care.
I cherish what I have
Had of the temporal:
I am no longer young
But the winds and waters are;
80 What falls away will fall;
All things bring me to love.

4

The breath of a long root,
The shy perimeter
Of the unfolding rose,
85 The green, the altered leaf,
The oyster's weeping foot,
And the incipient star—
Are part of what she is.
She wakes the ends of life.

90 Being myself, I sing
The soul's immediate joy.
Light, light, where's my repose?
A wind wreathes round a tree.
A thing is done: a thing
95 Body and spirit know
When I do what she does:
Creaturely creature, she!—

I kiss her moving mouth,
Her swart hilarious skin;
100 She breaks my breath in half;
She frolicks like a beast;
And I dance round and round,
A fond and foolish man,
And see and suffer myself
105 In another being, at last.

THE VOICE

One feather is a bird,
I claim; one tree, a wood;
In her low voice I heard
More than a mortal should;
5 And so I stood apart,
Hidden in my own heart.

And yet I roamed out where
Those notes went, like the bird,
Whose thin song hung in air,
10 Diminished, yet still heard:
I lived with open sound,
Aloft, and on the ground.

That ghost was my own choice,
The shy cerulean bird;
15 It sang with her true voice,
And it was I who heard
A slight voice reply;
I heard; and only I.

Desire exults the ear:
20 Bird, girl, and ghostly tree,
The earth, the solid air—
Their slow song sang in me;
The long noon pulsed away,
Like any summer day.

THE OTHER

What is she, while I live?—
Who plagues me with her Shape,
Lifting a nether Lip
Lightly: so buds unleave;
5 But if I move too close,
Who busks me on the Nose?

Is she what I become?
Is this my final Face?
I find her every place;
10 She happens, time on time—
My Nose feels for my Toe;
Nature's too much to know.

Who can surprise a thing
Or come to love alone?
15 A lazy natural man,
I loll, I loll, all Tongue.
She moves, and I adore:
Motion can do no more.

A child stares past a fire
20 With the same absent gaze:
I know her careless ways!—
Desire hides from desire.
Aging, I sometimes weep,
Yet still laugh in my sleep.

THE SENSUALISTS

"There is no place to turn," she said,
  "You have me pinned so close;
My hair's all tangled on your head,
  My back is just one bruise;
5 I feel we're breathing with the dead;
  O angel, let me loose!"

And she was right, for there beside
  The gin and cigarettes,
A woman stood, pure as a bride,
10   Affrighted from her wits,
And breathing hard, as that man rode
  Between those lovely tits.

"My shoulder's bitten from your teeth;
  What's that peculiar smell?
15 No matter which one is beneath,
  Each is an animal,"—
The ghostly figure sucked its breath,
  And shuddered toward the wall;
Wrapped in the tattered robe of death,
20   It tiptoed down the hall.

"The bed itself begins to quake,
  I hate this sensual pen;
My neck, if not my heart, will break
  If we do this again,"—
25 Then each fell back, limp as a sack,
  Into the world of men.

SLUG

How I loved one like you when I was little!—
With his stripes of silver and his small house on his back,
Making a slow journey around the well-curb.
I longed to be like him, and was,
5 In my way, close cousin
To the dirt, my knees scrubbing
The gravel, my nose wetter than his.

When I slip, just slightly, in the dark,
I know it isn't a wet leaf,
10 But you, loose toe from the old life,
The cold slime come into being,
A fat, five-inch appendage
Creeping slowly over the wet grass,
Eating the heart out of my garden.

15 And you refuse to die decently!—
Flying upward through the knives of my lawnmower
Like pieces of smoked eel or raw oyster,
And I go faster in my rage to get done with it,
Until I'm scraping and scratching at you, on the doormat,
20 The small dead pieces sticking under an instep;
Or, poisoned, dragging a white skein of spittle over a path—
Beautiful, in its way, like quicksilver—
You shrink to something less,
A rain-drenched fly or spider.

25 I'm sure I've been a toad, one time or another.
With bats, weasels, worms—I rejoice in the kinship.
Even the caterpillar I can love, and the various vermin.
But as for you, most odious—
Would Blake call you holy?

MEDITATIONS OF AN OLD WOMAN

I'M HERE

1

Is it enough?—
The sun loosening the frost on December windows,
The glitter of wet in the first of morning?
The sound of voices, young voices, mixed with sleighbells,
5 Coming across snow in early evening?

Outside, the same sparrows bicker in the eaves.
I'm tired of tiny noises:
The April cheeping, the vireo's insistence,
The prattle of the young no longer pleases.
10 Behind the child's archness
Lurks the bad animal.

—How needles and corners perplex me!
   Dare I shrink to a hag,
   The worst surprise a corner could have,
15   A witch who sleeps with her horse?
   Some fates are worse.

2

I was queen of the vale—
For a short while,
Living all my heart's summer alone,
20 Ward of my spirit,
Running through high grasses,
My thighs brushing against flower-crowns;

Leaning, out of all breath,
Bracing my back against a sapling,
25 Making it quiver with my body;
At the stream's edge, trailing a vague finger;
Flesh-awkward, half-alive,
Fearful of high places, in love with horses;
In love with stuffs, silks,
30 Rubbing my nose in the wool of blankets;
Bemused; pleased to be;
Mindful of cries,
The meaningful whisper,
The wren, the catbird.

35   So much of adolescence is an ill-defined dying,
    An intolerable waiting,
    A longing for another place and time,
    Another condition.

I stayed: a willow to the wind.
40 The bats twittered at noon.
The swallows flew in and out of the smokeless chimneys.
I sang to the edges of flame,
My skin whiter in the soft weather,
My voice softer.

3

45 I remember walking down a path,
Down wooden steps toward a weedy garden;
And my dress caught on a rose-brier.
When I bent to untangle myself,
The scent of the half-opened buds came up over me.
50 I thought I was going to smother.

    In the slow coming-out of sleep,
    On the sill of the eyes, something flutters,
    A thing we feel at evening, and by doors,
    Or when we stand at the edge of a thicket,
55   And the ground-chill comes closer to us,
    From under the dry leaves,
    A beachy wetness.

The body, delighting in thresholds,
Rocks in and out of itself.
60   A bird, small as a leaf,
Sings in the first
Sunlight.

And the time I was so sick—
The whole place shook whenever I got a chill—
65 I closed my eyes, and saw small figures dancing,
A congress of tree-shrews and rats,
Romping around a fire,
Jumping up and down on their hind feet,
Their forepaws joined together, like hands—
70 They seemed very happy.

In my grandmother's inner eye,
So she told me when I was little,
A bird always kept singing.
She was a serious woman.

4

75 My geranium is dying, for all I can do,
Still leaning toward the last place the sun was.
I've tried I don't know how many times to replant it.
But these roses: I can wear them by looking away.
The eyes rejoice in the act of seeing and the fresh after-image;
80 Without staring like a lout, or a moping adolescent;
Without commotion.

Look at the far trees at the end of the garden.
The flat branch of that hemlock holds the last of the sun,
Rocking it, like a sun-struck pond,
85 In a light wind.

I prefer the still joy:
The wasp drinking at the edge of my cup;
A snake lifting its head;
A snail's music.

90 What's weather to me? Even carp die in this river.
I need a pond with small eels. And a windy orchard.
I'm no midge of that and this. The dirt glitters like salt.
Birds are around. I've all the singing I would.
I'm not far from a stream.
95 It's not my first dying.
I can hold this valley,
Loose in my lap,
In my arms.

If the wind means me,
100   I'm here!
Here.

MEDITATIONS OF AN OLD WOMAN

FOURTH MEDITATION

1

I was always one for being alone,
Seeking in my own way, eternal purpose;
At the edge of the field waiting for the pure moment;
Standing, silent, on sandy beaches or walking along green embankments;
5 Knowing the sinuousness of small waters:
As a chip or shell, floating lazily with a slow current,
A drop of the night rain still in me,
A bit of water caught in a wrinkled crevice,
A pool riding and shining with the river,
10 Dipping up and down in the ripples,
Tilting back the sunlight.

Was it yesterday I stretched out the thin bones of my innocence?
O the songs we hide, singing only to ourselves!
Once I could touch my shadow, and be happy;
15 In the white kingdoms, I was light as a seed,
Drifting with the blossoms,
A pensive petal.

But a time comes when the vague life of the mouth no longer suffices;
The dead make more impossible demands from their silence;
20 The soul stands, lonely in its choice,
Waiting, itself a slow thing,
In the changing body.

The river moves, wrinkled by midges,
A light wind stirs in the pine needles.
25 The shape of a lark rises from a stone;
But there is no song.

2

What is it to be a woman?
To be contained, to be a vessel?
To prefer a window to a door?
30 A pool to a river?
To become lost in a love,
Yet remain only half aware of the intransient glory?
To be a mouth, a meal of meat?
To gaze at a face with the fixed eyes of a spaniel?

35 I think of the self-involved:
The ritualists of the mirror, the lonely drinkers,
The minions of benzedrine and paraldehyde,
And those who submerge themselves deliberately in trivia,
Women who become their possessions,
40 Shapes stiffening into metal,
Match-makers, arrangers of picnics—
What do their lives mean,
And the lives of their children?—
The young, brow-beaten early into a baleful silence,
45 Frozen by a father's lip, a mother's failure to answer.
Have they seen, ever, the sharp bones of the poor?
Or known, once, the soul's authentic hunger,
Those cat-like immaculate creatures
For whom the world works?

50 What do they need?
O more than a roaring boy,

For the sleek captains of intuition cannot reach them;
They feel neither the tearing iron
Nor the sound of another footstep—
55 How I wish them awake!
May the high flower of the hay climb into their hearts;
May they lean into light and live;
May they sleep in robes of green, among the ancient ferns;
May their eyes gleam with the first dawn;
60 May the sun gild them a worm;
May they be taken by the true burning;
May they flame into being!—

I see them as figures walking in a greeny garden,
Their gait formal and elaborate, their hair a glory,
65 The gentle and beautiful still-to-be-born;
The descendants of the playful tree-shrew that survived the archaic killers,
The fang and the claw, the club and the knout, the irrational edict,
The fury of the hate-driven zealot, the meanness of the human weasel;
Who turned a corner in time, when at last he grew a thumb;
70 A prince of small beginnings, enduring the slow stretches of change,
Who spoke first in the coarse short-hand of the subliminal depths,
Made from his terror and dismay a grave philosophical language;
A lion of flame, pressed to the point of love,
Yet moves gently among the birds.

3

75 Younglings, the small fish keep heading into the current.
What's become of care? This lake breathes like a rose.
Beguile me, change. What have I fallen from?
I drink my tears in a place where all light comes.
I'm in love with the dead! My whole forehead's a noise!
80 On a dark day I walk straight toward the rain.
Who else sweats light from a stone?
By singing we defend;
The husk lives on, ardent as a seed;
My back creaks with the dawn.
85 Is my body speaking? I breathe what I am:
The first and last of all things.
Near the graves of the great dead,
Even the stones speak.

THE LONGING

1

On things asleep, no balm:
A kingdom of stinks and sighs,
Fetor of cockroaches, dead fish, petroleum,
Worse than castoreum of mink or weasels,
5 Saliva dripping from warm microphones,
Agony of crucifixion on barstools.
      Less and less the illuminated lips,
      Hands active, eyes cherished;
      Happiness left to dogs and children—
10   (Matters only a saint mentions!)
Lust fatigues the soul.
How to transcend this sensual emptiness?
(Dreams drain the spirit if we dream too long.)
In a bleak time, when a week of rain is a year,
15 The slag-heaps fume at the edge of the raw cities:
The gulls wheel over their singular garbage;
The great trees no longer shimmer;
Not even the soot dances.

And the spirit fails to move forward,
20 But shrinks into a half-life, less than itself,
Falls back, a slug, a loose worm
Ready for any crevice,
An eyeless starer.

2

A wretch needs his wretchedness. Yes.
25 O pride, thou art a plume upon whose head?
How comprehensive that felicity! . . .

A body with the motion of a soul.
What dream's enough to breathe in? A dark dream.
The rose exceeds, the rose exceeds us all.
30 Who'd think the moon could pare itself so thin?
A great flame rises from the sunless sea;
The light cries out, and I am there to hear—
I'd be beyond; I'd be beyond the moon,
Bare as a bud, and naked as a worm.

35 To this extent I'm a stalk.
     —How free; how all alone.
Out of these nothings
     —All beginnings come.

3

I would with the fish, the blackening salmon, and the mad lemmings,
40 The children dancing, the flowers widening.
Who sighs from far away?
I would unlearn the lingo of exasperation, all the distortions of malice
                and hatred;
I would believe my pain: and the eye quiet on the growing rose;
I would delight in my hands, the branch singing, altering the excessive bird;
45 I long for the imperishable quiet at the heart of form;
I would be a stream, winding between great striated rocks in late summer;
A leaf, I would love the leaves, delighting in the redolent disorder of this
                mortal life,
This ambush, this silence,
Where shadow can change into flame,
50 And the dark be forgotten.
I have left the body of the whale, but the mouth of the night is still wide;
On the Bullhead, in the Dakotas, where the eagles eat well,
In the country of few lakes, in the tall buffalo grass at the base of the
                clay buttes,
In the summer heat, I can smell the dead buffalo,
55 The stench of their damp fur drying in the sun,
The buffalo chips drying.

      Old men should be explorers?
      I'll be an Indian.
      Iroquois.

JOURNEY TO THE INTERIOR

1

In the long journey out of the self,
There are many detours, washed-out interrupted raw places
Where the shale slides dangerously
And the back wheels hang almost over the edge
5 At the sudden veering, the moment of turning.
Better to hug close, wary of rubble and falling stones.
The arroyo cracking the road, the wind-bitten buttes, the canyons,
Creeks swollen in midsummer from the flash-flood roaring into the narrow
valley.

Reeds beaten flat by wind and rain,
10 Gray from the long winter, burnt at the base in late summer.
—Or the path narrowing,
Winding upward toward the stream with its sharp stones,
The upland of alder and birchtrees,
Through the swamp alive with quicksand,
15 The way blocked at last by a fallen fir-tree,
The thickets darkening,
The ravines ugly.

66

2

I remember how it was to drive in gravel,
Watching for dangerous down-hill places, where the wheels whined
                                                    beyond eighty—
20 When you hit the deep pit at the bottom of the swale,
The trick was to throw the car sideways and charge over the hill, full of
                                                    the throttle.
Grinding up and over the narrow road, spitting and roaring.
A chance? Perhaps. But the road was part of me, and its ditches,
And the dust lay thick on my eyelids,—Who ever wore goggles?—
25 Always a sharp turn to the left past a barn close to the roadside,
To a scurry of small dogs and a shriek of children,
The highway ribboning out in a straight thrust to the North,
To the sand dunes and fish flies, hanging, thicker than moths,
Dying brightly under the street lights sunk in coarse concrete,
30 The towns with their high pitted road-crowns and deep gutters,
Their wooden stores of silvery pine and weather-beaten red courthouses,
An old bridge below with a buckled iron railing, broken by some idiot
                                                    plunger;
Underneath, the sluggish water running between weeds, broken wheels,
                                                    tires, stones.

And all flows past—
35 The cemetery with two scrubby trees in the middle of the prairie,
The dead snakes and muskrats, the turtles gasping in the rubble,
The spikey purple bushes in the winding dry creek bed—
The floating hawks, the jackrabbits, the grazing cattle—
I am not moving but they are,
40 And the sun comes out of a blue cloud over the Tetons,
While, farther away, the heat-lightning flashes.
I rise and fall in the slow sea of a grassy plain,
The wind veering the car slightly to the right,
Whipping the line of white laundry, bending the cottonwoods apart,
45 The scraggly wind-break of a dusty ranch-house.
I rise and fall, and time folds
Into a long moment;
And I hear the lichen speak,
And the ivy advance with its white lizard feet—
50 On the shimmering road,
On the dusty detour.

3

I see the flower of all water, above and below me, the never receding,
Moving, unmoving in a parched land, white in the moonlight:
The soul at a still-stand,
55 At ease after rocking the flesh to sleep,
Petals and reflections of petals mixed on the surface of a glassy pool,
And the waves flattening out when the fishermen drag their nets over the
stones.

In the moment of time when the small drop forms, but does not fall,
I have known the heart of the sun,—
60 In the dark and light of a dry place,
In a flicker of fire brisked by a dusty wind.
I have heard, in a drip of leaves,
A slight song,
After the midnight cries.
65 I rehearse myself for this:
The stand at the stretch in the face of death,
Delighting in surface change, the glitter of light on waves,
And I roam elsewhere, my body thinking,
Turning toward the other side of light,
70 In a tower of wind, a tree idling in air,
Beyond my own echo,
Neither forward nor backward,
Unperplexed, in a place leading nowhere.

As a blind man, lifting a curtain, knows it is morning,
75 I know this change:
On one side of silence there is no smile;
But when I breathe with the birds,
The spirit of wrath becomes the spirit of blessing,
And the dead begin from their dark to sing in my sleep.

THE ROSE

1

There are those to whom place is unimportant,
But this place, where sea and fresh water meet,
Is important—
Where the hawks sway out into the wind,
5 Without a single wingbeat,
And the eagles sail low over the fir trees,
And the gulls cry against the crows
In the curved harbors,
And the tide rises up against the grass
10 Nibbled by sheep and rabbits.

A time for watching the tide,
For the heron's hieratic fishing,
For the sleepy cries of the towhee,
The morning birds gone, the twittering finches,
15 But still the flash of the kingfisher, the wingbeat of the scoter,
The sun a ball of fire coming down over the water,
The last geese crossing against the reflected afterlight,
The moon retreating into a vague cloud-shape
To the cries of the owl, the eerie whooper.
20 The old log subsides with the lessening waves,
And there is silence.

I sway outside myself
Into the darkening currents,
Into the small spillage of driftwood,
25 The waters swirling past the tiny headlands.
Was it here I wore a crown of birds for a moment
While on a far point of the rocks
The light heightened,
And below, in a mist out of nowhere,
30 The first rain gathered?

2

As when a ship sails with a light wind—
The waves less than the ripples made by rising fish,
The lacelike wrinkles of the wake widening, thinning out,

Sliding away from the traveler's eye,
35 The prow pitching easily up and down,
The whole ship rolling slightly sideways,
The stern high, dipping like a child's boat in a pond—
Our motion continues.

But this rose, this rose in the sea-wind,
40 Stays,
Stays in its true place,
Flowering out of the dark,
Widening at high noon, face upward,
A single wild rose, struggling out of the white embrace of the morning-
glory,
45 Out of the briary hedge, the tangle of matted underbrush,
Beyond the clover, the ragged hay,
Beyond the sea pine, the oak, the wind-tipped madrona,
Moving with the waves, the undulating driftwood,
Where the slow creek winds down to the black sand of the shore
50 With its thick grassy scum and crabs scuttling back into their glistening
craters.

And I think of roses, roses,
White and red, in the wide six-hundred-foot greenhouses,

And my father standing astride the cement benches,
Lifting me high over the four-foot stems, the Mrs. Russells, and his own
elaborate hybrids,
55 And how those flowerheads seemed to flow toward me, to beckon me,
only a child, out of myself.

What need for heaven, then,
With that man, and those roses?

3

What do they tell us, sound and silence?
I think of American sounds in this silence:
60 On the banks of the Tombstone, the wind-harps having their say,
The thrush singing alone, that easy bird,
The killdeer whistling away from me,
The mimetic chortling of the catbird
Down in the corner of the garden, among the raggedy lilacs,
65 The bobolink skirring from a broken fencepost,
The bluebird, lover of holes in old wood, lilting its light song,
And that thin cry, like a needle piercing the ear, the insistent cicada,
And the ticking of snow around oil drums in the Dakotas,
The thin whine of telephone wires in the wind of a Michigan winter,
70 The shriek of nails as old shingles are ripped from the top of a roof,
The bulldozer backing away, the hiss of the sandblaster,
And the deep chorus of horns coming up from the streets in early morning.
I return to the twittering of swallows above water,
And that sound, that single sound,
75 When the mind remembers all,
And gently the light enters the sleeping soul,
A sound so thin it could not woo a bird,

Beautiful my desire, and the place of my desire.

I think of the rock singing, and light making its own silence,
80 At the edge of a ripening meadow, in early summer,
The moon lolling in the close elm, a shimmer of silver,
Or that lonely time before the breaking of morning
When the slow freight winds along the edge of the ravaged hillside,
And the wind tries the shape of a tree,
85 While the moon lingers,

And a drop of rain water hangs at the tip of a leaf
Shifting in the wakening sunlight
Like the eye of a new-caught fish.

4

I live with the rocks, their weeds,
90 Their filmy fringes of green, their harsh
Edges, their holes
Cut by the sea-slime, far from the crash
Of the long swell,
The oily, tar-laden walls
95 Of the toppling waves,
Where the salmon ease their way into the kelp beds,
And the sea rearranges itself among the small islands.

Near this rose, in this grove of sun-parched, wind-warped madronas,
Among the half-dead trees, I came upon the true ease of myself,
100 As if another man appeared out of the depths of my being,
And I stood outside myself,
Beyond becoming and perishing,
A something wholly other,
As if I swayed out on the wildest wave alive,
105 And yet was still.
And I rejoiced in being what I was:
In the lilac change, the white reptilian calm,
In the bird beyond the bough, the single one
With all the air to greet him as he flies,
110 The dolphin rising from the darkening waves;

And in this rose, this rose in the sea-wind,
Rooted in stone, keeping the whole of light,
Gathering to itself sound and silence—
Mine and the sea-wind's.

HER LONGING

Before this longing,
I lived serene as a fish,
At one with the plants in the pond,
The mare's tail, the floating frogbit,
5 Among my eight-legged friends,
Open like a pool, a lesser parsnip,
Like a leech, looping myself along,
A bug-eyed edible one,
A mouth like a stickleback,—
10 A thing quiescent!

But now—
The wild stream, the sea itself cannot contain me:
I dive with the black hag, the cormorant,
Or walk the pebbly shore with the humpbacked heron,
15 Shaking out my catch in the morning sunlight,
Or rise with the gar-eagle, the great-winged condor,
Floating over the mountains,
Pitting my breast against the rushing air,
A phoenix, sure of my body,
20 Perpetually rising out of myself,
My wings hovering over the shorebirds,
Or beating against the black clouds of the storm,
Protecting the sea-cliffs.

HER TIME

When all
My waterfall
Fancies sway away
From me, in the sea's silence;
5 In the time
When the tide moves
Neither forward nor back,
And the small waves
Begin rising whitely,
10 And the quick winds
Flick over the close whitecaps,
And two scoters fly low,
Their four wings beating together,
And my salt-laden hair
15 Flies away from my face
Before the almost invisible
Spray, and the small shapes
Of light on the far
Cliff disappear in a last
20 Glint of the sun, before
The long surf of the storm booms
Down on the near shore,
When everything—birds, men, dogs—
Runs to cover:
25 I'm one to follow,
To follow.

LIGHT LISTENED

O what could be more nice
Than her ways with a man?
She kissed me more than twice
Once we were left alone.
5 Who'd look when he could feel?
She'd more sides than a seal.

The close air faintly stirred.
Light deepened to a bell,
The love-beat of a bird.
10 She kept her body still
And watched the weather flow.
We live by what we do.

All's known, all, all around:
The shape of things to be;
15 A green thing loves the green
And loves the living ground.
The deep shade gathers night;
She changed with changing light.

We met to leave again
20 The time we broke from time;
A cold air brought its rain,
The singing of a stem.
She sang a final song;
Light listened when she sang.

THE HAPPY THREE

Inside, my darling wife
Sharpened a butcher knife;
Sighed out her pure relief
      That I was gone.

5 When I had tried to clean
My papers up, between
Words skirting the obscene—
      She frowned her frown.

Shelves have a special use;
10 And Why muddy shoes
In with your underclothes?
      She asked, woman.

So I betook myself
With not one tiny laugh
15 To drink some half-and-half
            On the back lawn.

Who should come up right then,
But our goose, Marianne,
Having escaped her pen,
20   Hunting the sun.

Named for a poetess,
(Whom I like none-the-less),
Her pure-white featheriness
            She paused to preen;

25 But when she pecked my toe,
My banked-up vertigo
Vanished like April snow;
            All rage was gone.

Then a close towhee, a
30 Phoebe not far away
Sang out audaciously
            Notes finely drawn.

Back to the house we ran,
Me, and dear Marianne—
35 Then we romped out again,
            Out again,
            Out again,
            Three in the sun.

THE SHY MAN

The full moon was shining upon the broad sea;
I sang to the one star that looked down at me;
I sang to the white horse that grazed on the quay,—
    As I walked by the high sea-wall.
5   But my lips they,
        My lips they,
    Said never a word,
    As I moped by the high sea-wall.

The curlew's slow night song came on the water.
10 That tremble of sweet notes set my heart astir,
As I walked beside her, the O'Connell's daughter,
    I knew that I did love her.
        But my lips they,
        My lips they,
15   Said never a word,
    As we walked by the high sea-wall.

The full moon has fallen, the night wind is down
And I lie here thinking in bleak Bofin town
I lie here and thinking, 'I am not alone.'
20   For here close beside me is O'Connell's daughter,
        And my lips they, my lips they,
        Say many a word,
    As we embrace by the high sea-wall.
        O! my lips they, my lips they,
25   Say many a word,
    As we kiss by the high sea-wall.

OTTO

1

He was the youngest son of a strange brood,
A Prussian who learned early to be rude
To fools and frauds: He does not put on airs
Who lived above a potting shed for years.
5 I think of him, and I think of his men,
As close to him as any kith or kin.
Max Laurisch had the greenest thumb of all.
A florist does not woo the beautiful:
He potted plants as if he hated them.
10 What root of his ever denied its stem?
When flowers grew, their bloom extended him.

2

His hand could fit into a woman's glove,
And in a wood he knew whatever moved;
Once when he saw two poachers on his land,
15 He threw his rifle over with one hand;
Dry bark flew in their faces from his shot,—
He always knew what he was aiming at.
They stood there with their guns; he walked toward,
Without his rifle, and slapped each one hard;
20 It was no random act, for those two men
Had slaughtered game, and cut young fir trees down.
I was no more than seven at the time.

3

A house for flowers! House upon house they built,
Whether for love or out of obscure guilt
25 For ancestors who loved a warlike show,
Or Frenchmen killed a hundred years ago,
And yet still violent men, whose stacked-up guns
Killed every cat that neared their pheasant runs;
When Hattie Wright's angora died as well,
30 My father took it to her, by the tail.
Who loves the small can be both saint and boor,
(And some grow out of shape, their seed impure;)
The Indians loved him, and the Polish poor.

4

In my mind's eye I see those fields of glass,
35 As I looked out at them from the high house,
Riding beneath the moon, hid from the moon,
Then slowly breaking whiter in the dawn;
When George the watchman's lantern dropped from sight
The long pipes knocked: it was the end of night.
40 I'd stand upon my bed, a sleepless child
Watching the waking of my father's world.—
O world so far away! O my lost world!

THE GERANIUM

When I put her out, once, by the garbage pail,
She looked so limp and bedraggled,
So foolish and trusting, like a sick poodle,
Or a wizened aster in late September,
5 I brought her back in again
For a new routine—
Vitamins, water, and whatever
Sustenance seemed sensible
At the time: she'd lived
10 So long on gin, bobbie pins, half-smoked cigars, dead beer,
Her shriveled petals falling
On the faded carpet, the stale
Steak grease stuck to her fuzzy leaves.
(Dried-out, she creaked like a tulip.)

15 The things she endured!—
The dumb dames shrieking half the night
Or the two of us, alone, both seedy,
Me breathing booze at her,
She leaning out of her pot toward the window.

20 Near the end, she seemed almost to hear me—
And that was scary—
So when that snuffling cretin of a maid
Threw her, pot and all, into the trash-can,
I said nothing.

25 But I sacked the presumptuous hag the next week,
I was that lonely.

THE PIKE

The river turns,
Leaving a place for the eye to rest,
A furred, a rocky pool,
A bottom of water.

5 The crabs tilt and eat, leisurely,
And the small fish lie, without shadow, motionless,
Or drift lazily in and out of the weeds.
The bottom-stones shimmer back their irregular striations,
And the half-sunken branch bends away from the gazer's eye

10 A scene for the self to abjure!—
And I lean, almost into the water,
My eye always beyond the surface reflection;
I lean, and love these manifold shapes,
Until, out from a dark cove,
15 From beyond the end of a mossy log,
With one sinuous ripple, then a rush,
A thrashing-up of the whole pool,
The pike strikes.

INFIRMITY

In purest song one plays the constant fool
As changes shimmer in the inner eye.
I stare and stare into a deepening pool
And tell myself my image cannot die.
5 I love myself: that's my one constancy.
Oh, to be something else, yet still to be!

Sweet Christ, rejoice in my infirmity;
There's little left I care to call my own.
Today they drained the fluid from a knee
10 And pumped a shoulder full of cortisone;
Thus I conform to my divinity
By dying inward, like an aging tree.

The instant ages on the living eye;
Light on its rounds, a pure extreme of light
15 Breaks on me as my meager flesh breaks down—
The soul delights in that extremity.
Blessed the meek; they shall inherit wrath;
I'm son and father of my only death.

A mind too active is no mind at all;
20 The deep eye sees the shimmer on the stone;
The eternal seeks, and finds, the temporal,
The change from dark to light of the slow moon,
Dead to myself, and all I hold most dear,
I move beyond the reach of wind and fire.

25 Deep in the greens of summer sing the lives
I've come to love. A vireo whets its bill.
The great day balances upon the leaves;
My ears still hear the bird when all is still;
My soul is still my soul, and still the Son,
30 And knowing this, I am not yet undone.

Things without hands take hands: there is no choice,—
Eternity's not easily come by.
When opposites come suddenly in place,
I teach my eyes to hear, my ears to see
35 How body from spirit slowly does unwind
Until we are pure spirit at the end.

THE DECISION

1

What shakes the eye but the invisible?
Running from God's the longest race of all.
A bird kept haunting me when I was young—
The phoebe's slow retreating from its song,
5 Nor could I put that sound out of my mind,
The sleepy sound of leaves in a light wind.

2

Rising or falling's all one discipline!
The line of my horizon's growing thin!
Which is the way? I cry to the dread black,
10 The shifting shade, the cinders at my back.
Which is the way? I ask, and turn to go,
As a man turns to face on-coming snow.

ONCE MORE, THE ROUND

What's greater, Pebble or Pond?
What can be known? The Unknown.
My true self runs toward a Hill
More! O More! visible.

5 Now I adore my life
With the Bird, the abiding Leaf,
With the Fish, the questing Snail,
And the Eye altering all;
And I dance with William Blake
10 For love, for Love's sake;

And everything comes to One,
As we dance on, dance on, dance on.

INDEX OF FIRST LINES AND TITLES

2 3 4 5 6 7 8 9 10 11 12 13 14 15 16 17 18 19 20 21 22 23 24 25   W   72 71 70 69